To Liz,

Merry Christmas

lots of love

Christopher

Christmas 99

CATCH THE
MILLENNIUM
BUG
WITH ERIC AND

SOUTHAMPTON

Edited by Carl Golder

First published in Great Britain in 1999 by
YOUNG WRITERS
Remus House,
Coltsfoot Drive,
Woodston,
Peterborough, PE2 9JX
Telephone (01733) 890066

HB ISBN 0 75431 586 X
SB ISBN 0 75431 587 8

FOREWORD

Young Writers have produced poetry books in conjunction with schools for over eight years; providing a platform for talented young people to shine. This year, the Celebration 2000 collection of regional anthologies were developed with the millennium in mind.

With the nation taking stock of how far we have come, and reflecting on what we want to achieve in the future, our anthologies give a vivid insight into the thoughts and experiences of the younger generation.

We were once again impressed with the quality and attention to detail of every entry received and hope you will enjoy the poems we have decided to feature in *Celebration 2000 Southampton* for many years to come.

CONTENTS

The Poems

MY WEEK AT THE THEME PARK

One day, me, my friend and his mum, went to
Paltons Park.

First we went and spent our money and bought
something funny.

Then we went on the go-karts and ate some
jam tarts.

We went on a big slide and went on a train ride.
We went on the games and some were the same.
We went on the water carts then we played darts.

That is the end of our weeks trip, now we're going
to have a kip.

Reece Williams (10) & Craig Baker (9)

IF I HAD A MILLION POUNDS

If I had a million pounds I could buy lots and lots of things
I could buy seven pairs of golden earrings.

I would buy a washing machine for Uncle Alf
and a chocolate factory for myself.

I would give my mum and dad a thousand pounds
and all day long play on school grounds.

Gemma Webb (10) & Carly Sparshott (9)

IF I HAD A MILLION-BILLION POUNDS!

If I had a million-billion pounds
I'd buy a chocolate factory
and I wouldn't share it with anybody.
If I had more money
I'd give some to my mummy.
Then I'd travel around the world
I'd buy a motorbike and even a rally car.
All day long I'd swim in my pool
I'd race with my friends.
But I'd keep all my money safe
In case a burglar tries to steal it!

Christopher Jepp & Liam Willcox (9)

IF I HAD ONE MILLION POUNDS

If I had one million pounds
I would spend it all at the mall.
I would buy a football and a diamond ring
A cockatoo and a teddy bear kangeroo.
I would buy loads of clothes and shoes
Loads of jewellery and make-up
and an adorable little pup.
I would buy lots of sweets
and ten pairs of sandals for my feet.
I would book a holiday
just to get away for fourteen days.
And when I come back from my holiday
I will probably wish I was still away.

Stacey Eden (9)

ANIMAL POEM

Cats:
Cats play with cotton balls
every day they purr and play.
Dogs:
Dogs they bark in the park
when it's dark.
They run for fun
with anyone.

Martin Cook (10)

I WENT DANCING ON THE BEACH

All night on the beach I was dancing,
I stopped to eat with sandals on my feet.
I had curry sauce on my chips,
with sausages cut into bits.
I had for dessert a strawberry sundae
with a cherry on top,
and a milkshake served right to the top.
I was very full, that's why I fell off my stool.
I got up again and wiped myself down
and walked out of the restaurant
and started dancing again.

Michael Chambers (10)

THE PAULTONS PARK TRIP

One day we went to Paultons Park
and I took my dog but
all he did was bark, bark, bark.

The first thing we went on was
the log ride.
The dog sat on the log like a giant hog
we all sat there with pride.

Then we had an unexplainable trip
we had so much fun that we needed some kip
and that was the end of the trip.

Leighann Gale & Amanda Zennodrajewski (10)

FOOTBALL ROCK HARD

Red card - Off you go!
Take your early shower.
You keep on kicking people's shins,
with all your football power.

Then they score a goal.
Like a trail of lava
the crowd erupts
like a volcano roaring.

The manager goes crazy
the explosion appears.
That's the end of all the tears.

Ryan Dickson & Richard Orman (10)

LOOPY LUCY

There was a lady called Lucy
but everyone called her Loopy Lucy
because she's so loopy she breaks everything around her.
She breaks plates, cups, saucers and everything you can imagine.
At work she behaves like a charm - but everyone doesn't think so.
So that's how she got a name called Loopy Lucy.

Martin Beesley (10)

WHAT'S IT LIKE BEING OLD?

What's it like being old?
I hope it's not boring - better not be!
Will I go grey and bald?
Find out in 70 years time - I'll be 80 then.
If I'm 10 years old now, 70 years doesn't seem far away.
I'm going to be old soon - oh no!

Graham Galton (9)

THE SOMETHING

The something is coming
It's jumping down the stair
The something is coming
It's flying through the air!

The something is large
The something is small
The something is hairy
It slithers up the wall.

The something is coming
It's jumping down the stair
The something is coming
It's bouncing through the air!

The something is gruesome
The something is sly
The something is fat
Although it can fly.

The something is coming
It's jumping down the stair
The something is coming
It's gliding through the air!

The something is crawling
The something is near
The something is sprawling
The something is . . . *here!*

Jenny Palmer & Becky Anderson (11)

SUMMER

I can hear chirping birds in the trees
I can see happy children playing outside
I can feel the breeze blowing from the trees
I can hear laughing children watching
Punch and Judy.
I can hear the sea crashing on the rocks,
I can see fluttering butterflies flying to and fro.

Lana Sinclair (8)

ANIMAL NOISES

A lion roars a mighty *roar,*
A gorilla beats its chest, like King Kong!
A snake hisses like a baby's rattle,
An elephant makes noises through its nose!
Monkeys talk to each other,
That's the jungle spirit.

Abigail Burchell (9)

COOL SUMMER

I can hear chuckling children laughing at Punch and Judy shows,
Gentle waves crashing against the rocks,
Dolphins gliding in the sea quickly.
I can see birds eating juicy worms
Crunching away while cats are eating their meals.
I can feel the dripping ice lollies on me,
I lick my lips
Then it's time to go home.

Daniel Orman (8)

SUMMER

I can feel the hot breeze coming,
and I'm feeling the summer.
When I feel the summer coming
I feel great.

I can see the beautiful sun,
I can see beautiful flowers
and I can see the pretty baby birds.
I can see lovely ice lollies too.

I can hear little children laughing,
I can hear trees swaying,
I can hear cats trying to catch rats
And mummies saying
'Dinner time.'

Jenna Burnett (7)

SPRING

This is the weather the cat likes
        And so do I.
When children are playing out later
        And so am I.

When squirrels are climbing up the trees
        And so am I.
When children are playing in their pools
        And so am I.

Michael Hegarty (8) & Jeraldine Baddams (7)

WEATHER

This is the weather the cat likes
      And so do I
When buds appear in swaying trees
When baby birds are born
Sweet daffodils sway in the breeze
      And so do I
This is the time when new animals are born
When animals come out of hibernation.

Simon Lane (7) & Nicky Brown (8)

AUTUMN

This is the weather the squirrels like
And so do I;
When squirrels collect nuts for hibernation
And leaves turn brown and fall onto the ground
And when people walk onto the leaves
They go crunch, crunch, crunch
And crackle and squelch in the mud
And children jump on the acorns at playtime
And so do I.

Sarah Louise Curtis (8)

SPRING

This is the weather the birds like
        And so do I.
When blossom appears on the trees
And rabbits bounce around
And school children skip to school
        And so do I.

Emma Saint (7)

AUTUMN

Autumn is the season I like
when leaves turn brown and flutter
to the ground
and when people tread on leaves they
crunch and crackle.
When the wind brushes against you
and the sunset goes down very slowly.

Hayleigh King (7)

WEATHER

This is the weather the seagull likes
And so do I.
When happy people visit the beach
When people look up into the wonderful sky
And grown-ups read fantasy rhymes
And children like to play in the sun.

Teachers teach children to write joyful fables
And children always have fun!
Tiny chestnuts fall off the pines.

Little toddlers begin to swim
Older children begin secondary school
And all the children are . . .
     Happy!

Michael Porter (7)

THE OLD HAUNTED HOUSE

In the haunted house the clock ticks slowly
When you open the door to the living room it squeaks.
When you walk up the stairs it creaks slowly
In the bedroom there is a box
Open the box there is a
Ghost!

Ryan McNeill (8)

WHEN I WENT TO THE ZOO

When I went to the zoo,
I saw a cute kangaroo
And then I saw a cockatoo.
They did not fly around,
But then the kangaroo sat on the ground.

I saw a baby ostrich,
I'll sell its eggs and become rich,
Then I will go and buy some chips.

Matthew Hunt (10)

TIM WHO WANTED EVERYTHING

There was a little boy called Tim,
Who always wanted everything.
Once he went to the Bargate Centre
And met a famous toy maker.

He had pogo sticks and plastic pharaohs,
But Tim bought a personal stereo
And when Tim finally got home,
He wanted to have a go.

But Tim forgot to get an adapter,
So he went back but couldn't find the maker,
So he borrowed one from Mum's big stereo,
It was a hard job though!

Suddenly the stereo fell on Tim,
It actually killed him.
His mum and dad heard the crash
And they found Tim squashed flat!

Adam Porter (9)

IF I HAD A MILLION POUNDS

If I had a million pounds
I'd have six girlfriends
Just like Henry VIII!
I would buy The Dell
And a marshmallow factory.

I'd buy Stamford Bridge
And I would play at Stamford Bridge
Until I score 100 *goals!*

I'd buy a nice car and a motorbike
And have a lovely cruise around the world!
I want to see Egypt, India, Greece and Brazil
And settle down in Australia
In the sun and swim in the warm blue seas!

Andreas Beirne (9) & Darryl Clarke (10)

WEATHER

This is the weather the cat loves
And so do I.
When daffodils sway in the open fields
And the baby birds start to fly
And lovely tulips begin to grow
And little buds appear on the trees
And children play in the grassy park
And so do I.

Stacey Kehoe (8)

WINTER

Winter is the season when animals hibernate and keep warm
When children play and make snowmen
And throw snowballs and have fun
And when children wear woolly hats and gloves
And when the days get shorter and the nights get longer.

Emma Jepp (8)

WEATHER

This is the weather the cat hates,
And so do I.
When trees are covered in snow
And the wind blows
And we sit in front of a hot fire
Cuddled up and warm.
The cat is feeling happy and safe
And so do I.

Florence Lo (7) & Charlene Lacey (8)

SUMMER

In summer I can hear people playing on the beach
and hear birds chirping in the swaying trees
and hear children swimming in the wavy sea.

I can see the blossom growing on the trees
and daffodils growing in the soil
and I can see all types of birds laying eggs
and finding juicy long worms for their babies.

I can feel the breeze blowing in my face
and I can feel the hot sun warming me up
and my friends and I feel quite cold and quite hot
And I love summer.

Sam Cooper (7)

WEATHER

This is the weather the dog likes
And so do I.
When children go out to play
And so do I.

This is the weather the cat hates
And so do I
And the cat gets wet
And so do I.

This is the weather the rabbit likes
And so do I.
When the rabbit goes out to find food
And so do I.

This is the weather the bird likes
And so do I.
When they tweet in the trees
And so do I.

Sophie Dewell (7)

SPRING

This is the weather the birds love
And so do I
When trees sway in the breeze
And blossom appears on the trees
And baby birds start to fly
And nestlings sigh
And so do I.

Alison Sanders (8)

A RAINY DAY

This is the weather the dads hate
And so do I
When the blossom is disappearing
And the leaves all die
And the children have fun inside
And mums all sigh
And dads go mad
And then the children are sad
And so am I.

Jamie-Lee Crow (8)

SUMMER

This is the weather the rabbit loves
And so do I.
When all the flowers bloom
And so do I.
When all the fruit grows
And so do I.
This is the weather the squirrel likes
And so do I.
When all the nuts and leaves fall off the trees
And blow around in the breeze
And so do I!

Karla Batchelor (7)

SUMMER

The sun shines in your face,
You keep on sweating all the time,
You go on holiday you need sunglasses,
It's really hot remember to take your suntan lotion.
It never gets very windy,
Sunbathing on the shore.
You have drinks all the time,
You go on walks that are really long,
Your socks always have a pong
If you wear them too long.
Your head gets dizzy as you get sums wrong.

Thomas Bishop *(7)*

LIONS

Running through the field
Prancing in the night
Nothing may stop this beast
It has a good sight.
Nothing can stop it I say
As it runs through the field
Roaring jumping it does
And soon it will be killed.

Shaun Gradidge (9)

FOOTBALL

Smelly socks
Dirty boots
People saying we won ten - nil
Year five feeling sad
Taking their clothes off
Getting dressed
Going home.

Luke Lovell (8)

HAMSTERS

Jumping rolling as he does
Rolling up in a ball of fuzz
Lovely and cosy, warm and snug
And he hates eating a slug
Then me, my mum and Warren go to a meeting
Then he runs and starts eating.
So we leave Squeaks alone
When we have gone
He fills his big cheeks.

Jasmine Lee (8)

SPRING IS FUN

Spring is fun, jumping about,
It's our freedom of spring
The new buds are on their way
Blossom on the trees is wonderful to see
It is beautiful when spring is here,
I love spring it is wonderful
People laughing, running through the flowers
Babies crying, sunshine bright
Teenagers running over the hills for shade
I don't know why they don't just find a tree,
Instead of going over the hills.
      Just remember
           Spring is fun.

Laura Baldacchino (8)

SUMMER

My birthday's in summer
When it's bright hot and clean
Summer is a fun season
But when I get sunburnt I scream.

Matthew Price (8)

CATS ABOUT

Cats lay around,
They lay in bed with you.
You give them food they purr at you.

It pounces back on your bed and goes to sleep,
It wakes up and stretches,
Starts to rise up.
It yawns and . . .
Falls off.
Might come back, might be lucky,
Yes! He's come back you're lucky.
He purrs and purrs
Pounces back
Oops he's fallen
He's fallen off my . . .
Lap.

Elizabeth Hall (9)

SPRING

Spring is full of colour
Spring is full of fun
It's my favourite season
And it's just begun.

Janine Dixon (9)

SPRING

S pring is comfy, nice and hot
P erfect for my baby sis to suck her thumb
R unning up and down the stairs
I lay under the sun
N ever ever get up
G od is near.

Nadia Petts (9)

FOOTBALL MAD

Today's the day we are out to play
A football match
Here we go we're on the field
Ready to start the game
We are down the wing again
And again
The whistle goes

It's
Half-time

We start the game again
Down the other end
The players are struggling
To get the ball out of the box
The whistle goes

It's
Full-time.
Back home again.

Justin Asher (9)

DAY POEM

Get up
Have a wash
Eat your breakfast
Wash your plates.
Get ready for school
Mum will take you
School bell rings
Go to class
Do some maths
Have a break
Go to English
Eat yummy lunch
Reading books
Science next
Three fifteen
Go home
Eat tea
Sleep.

Gemma O'Dell (9)

SPRING

Spring is coming, soon it will be here
If we go to the forest we might see deer
Flowers will be growing, blossoms on the trees
In the flowers we see some bumblebees
Easter is also in spring
And all the church bells ring
Days with the sun and light nights
Like a man with a bright light
Butterflies and wasps and a big bright sun
Lots of fun children having great fun
Sunbathing on the beach
Children playing on the street with tasty treats.

Andrew Gradidge & Hayleigh Lebbern (9)

SPRING

S wallows come back to Britain along with the cuckoos
P lant vegetables and flowers which will grow to eat
R ubber dinghies in the water floating along the seabed
I ce-cream for everyone
N o more rain but lots of sun
G oing to the beach every day.

James Clark (8)

SPRING

S ummer is almost here
P retty flowers like bright sunshine
R ainbows fading away
I ce-cream dripping off the cone
N ice air rising
G ood spring I love you spring.

Ashley Bran (9)

SPRING

S mall buds grow into leaves at spring
P lants and flowers and red roses grow in spring
R ed roses are bright and beautiful
I gloos are melting
N ights are getting shorter
G rowing wheat and corn.

C J Fredericks & Thomas Mason (9)

SPRINGTIME

F un times every day
L ovely flowers everywhere
O pal flowers sprouting up
W ild flowers like primroses
E els playing in the water
R ipe fruits to eat.
S unshine shining down on us.

Dale Davis (9)

SPRING

S pring grows beautiful flowers such as bluebells and snowdrops
P otatoes growing underground
R oast potatoes are grown every day
I ce-cream is lovely and cold
N ights are getting shorter
G rowing trees get wonderful buds which grow into trees
T he leaves are getting greener
I n spring is starts to get warmer
M ay flowers are grown
E very bird builds a nest and lays eggs.

Steven Agostinelli (8)

SPRINGTIME

S ummer is near
R ain comes and goes
P lants blossom and grow
I ce-cream needed in the hot sun
N o puddles left
G oing out
T ulips to be watered
I ndoors goes past
M ake mats for sunbathing
E nergy needed very fast.

Chantelle Hatcher (8) & Leanne Dobbing (9)

SPRING

S pringtime is nice
P retty daffodils everywhere
R ed flowers in your garden
I ce-cream all around
N ights are getting longer
G ood spring, I love you spring.

Rosy Bowers (8)

THE RIDE

I'm not scared of rides it's just silly rides
I'm not scared of rides
Let's go on this one OK
Up, up, up we go in the cave
Someone's got me it's just me
Round we go here's the big drop
The big drop
Ah ah ah I'm scared
I'm scared of rides.

Jason Hargood (10)

THE HAUNTED CASTLE

I saw a castle that had leaves covering it
I went in and the door closed up behind me
There was slime everywhere
The clock slowly stopped
I felt like there were ghosts everywhere all around me
I crept up the stairs it's the scariest place I've ever been
I went in the bedroom and I felt I would never be seen
        again.

Adam Kater (7)

HOME

Come home from school
Dress for play
Game of football
Score a goal - hooray
In at seven
PlayStation time
Spaghetti and sauce.

Craig Baddams (8)

FOOTBALL

Football is the best,
we love it all the time.
Football is the best,
just like lemon and lime.

Football is the best,
when we score a goal.
Football is the best,
with all our heart and soul.

Football is the best,
Man U and the rest.
Football is the best,
puts the players to the test.

David Kehoe, Richard Maunders & Daniel Glasspool (11)

THE MILLENNIUM

Now the millennium is here,
Let everybody raise a cheer.
This is the time to celebrate,
With a party that will be great.

As we greet the new dawn,
A new century will be born.
Let us hope it is a peaceful time,
Come and raise your glass with mine.

Let us hope that there is no war,
No starvation and more help to the poor;
Africa sees no more drought,
It's time to help each other out.

A new century starts right here,
A time to live without fear.
Now it's time to start again;
Health and happiness and no more pain.

Let us rebuild this special place,
And not discriminate against race.
Let us help the frail and the old;
That will mean more than any gold.

Let the new year fill you with joy,
For every man, woman, girl or boy.
The new millennium has begun,
Let us make sure it's filled with fun!

Kayleigh Richardson (10)

THE MILLENNIUM

As people stand in the cold frost,
They wait impatiently for the clock to strike 12.
As it chimes 12 times,
The people rejoice all over England and Wales.
Streamers in the air,
Flags up high,
Never stop until they touch the sky.
The millennium has come,
It's the 21st century,
People kissing under trees,
Many have come from all around
To see their families, who are really proud.
The day after people sit down,
After their hangover from drinking too much.
Still the beer is pulled out for a last holiday cheer,
A sign to show the brand new year!
But still we remember, 2000 years ago,
That Christ our Saviour was born complete with head and toes.

Sarah Varley (11)

SPACE

Into Space I will go,
I will see the stars
And Venus glow!

I'll race up and up,
Up to the top,
And then jump down with a clop, clop, clop!

Hannah Withington (9)

JUNGLE

In the jungle you can hear animals
running far and near.

You can hear the water dripping as the
rain is ripping.

You can hear the music drumming as
the animals start running.

You can feel the rumble at your feet and the
sun letting out its heat.

You can feel the bang as your feet hit
the sand.

In the jungle it's a scary place, you better
run at a great pace.

Gemma Fanstone (10)

RACISM

People call me names
just because I am black,
but I would not say nasty things
because they will just reflect back.

People call me chocolate boy,
and I don't find it funny,
I just think they are stupid people
with noses that are runny.

Now I know I should not say that
because they will just reflect back,
but I don't see any difference
between white people, brown and black.

Taran Missen (10)

LEAVES

Leaves are on trees
they can be big
they can be small
they can be green
they can turn brown

Along comes the wind
hurling and whirling
then down come the leaves
swishing with the breeze

Along come some children
crunch, crunch, scrunch, scrunch,
all the leaves are broken.

Anna Peskett (10)

THE SUN AND THE MOON

As hot as the sun
As thick as snow
As big as it can grow!

As wet as water
As soft as silk
As smooth as milk!

As bright as a light
On the moon it's full of gloom
The sun and the moon!

Emma Wells (10)

MILLENNIUM!

Tickety, tickety tock,
2000 struck the clock,
Everyone laughed and were
Full of cheer to welcome
in the . . .
        2000
          year.

Danielle O'prey (11)

MY MILLENNIUM INVENTIONS!

A new species found,
A pen with a brain,
A planet that we'd live on,
A solar-powered train.

A man-eating flower,
X-ray vision eyes,
A rainbow's new colour
A tall tower to climb.

A live talking robot,
A firework with a loud fizz
A common cold cure
But I hope it will stay just as it is!

Georgia Swain (11)

WINNIE THE POOH'S FRIEND, TIGGER

Tigger bounces around all day
Unlike Pooh who's as still as hay.
Tigger's rather springy too,
I'm surprised he doesn't keep needing the loo.
But Tigger has his special ways,
Like he has his own good days.

Rebecca Louise Williams (9)

THE ELEPHANT AND THE MONKEY

The elephant lived in India
it trampled all over the ground,
Everybody complained,
because of its terrible sound.

Along came the monkey,
all hairy, tall and brown.
The monkey looked up to the elephant
and said 'Stop making that sound.'

They both lived together,
as happy as can be.
I know this story
because the elephant was me.

Claire Viewing (9)

My Friend The Moon

As I lie in my bed at night
And watch the moon so big and bright
I see a face and think, oh please
Are you really made of cheese?

You light the sky that seems so bare
Bringing comfort as I stare
My eyes grow heavy, I must sleep
And pray to God my soul to keep.

When I awake, it will be bright
But still my thoughts are you and night.

Laurel Marston (10)

LIFE

Life is a ball of string,
you don't know where it starts or ends,
it is long, as long as can be,
it is short, as short as me,
you never know for evermore,
never,
never,
never,
will you know what life is,
never.

Andrew Corby (10)

THE DRAGON

Fiery breath has the dragon, giant wings
and tail, as he roars in anger when the ships sail.

His big red eyes stare in anger at the people's town,
as he flies above ready to come down.

But now the dragon is dead, we still tell
stories from our head, so may the dragon
rest in peace in its lonely bed.

Brooke Murray (10)

KING OF THE CLOUDS

If I was King of the Clouds
I would rain all day and night,
I would stop the sun from shining,
And I would feel alright.

If I was King of the Clouds
I would float around all day,
And never stop raining,
I want to rain all day, I wish, I pray.

If I was King of the Clouds
I would be very proud,
I can't believe I am
A white, fluffy cloud.

Ryan Freeman (9)

THE WHALE AND ME

The first time I saw him, he came up
like the rising of the sun.
I saw him jump over the shadow of the sun.
Then . . . he went to the bottom of the deep blue sea.
The next day I saw him with another whale,
but, the whale seemed to go away from him.
And then a sound came from him,
it seemed to me that he was crying.
So I went up to the sea and listened for a while,
then, I think that he noticed me
and something strange happened.
This time, he didn't swim away,
he came up to me, I could see that he was crying.
So I went for a step in life,
I went up to him and stroked his back,
and said that I would be his friend forever,
but, over the years he began to get older.
One day, it happened, when I called for him,
he didn't come.
All I could see was a body lying on the rocks,
I said goodbye and let him rest, in peace.

Joshua Jones (11)

YEAR 2000

Let's make a row!
The time is now!
Let's stand in line
The bells will chime
Throw your streamers in the air
Jump around like you don't care
A thousand years have just gone by
Some will laugh and some will cry
Some will look with a forward gaze
Some will remember with a misty haze
Men in suits will wear a frown
Will all their computers come crashing down?
For a passing minute we'll shout and scream
But at the end of the day, what does it mean?

Hanna Lutley (10)

THE COUNTDOWN TO 2000!

It's quarter-past ten, time to get ready,
my friends are coming round, better hide my teddy.

11 o'clock, the guests are all arriving,
Joe's drinking beer, he better not be driving.

5 to 12, everybody's here,
in 5 minutes we will all cheer.

We're having so much fun.

1, 2, 3,
Millennium!

Joanne Earl (11)

COLOURS

Purple
Plums are juicy fruits,
butterflies are colourful,
feathers are fluffy.

Orange
The summer is bright,
it is like a round pumpkin,
candles are scented.

Red
Like a traffic light,
it is like a big poppy,
like a strawberry.

Green
It is like a lime,
it is a juicy apple,
it is like the sea.

Gemma Murray (10)

THE BEACH

When I went to the beach,
It was nice and hot.
But when I went into the water, I shivered.
I went back on the beach to sunbathe in the sun,
But when I laid down, a crab pinched my nose.

I've had a nice day at the beach,
But now I have to go home.
I'll probably come back tomorrow,
I hope it doesn't rain.

Rosie Fox (9)

THE MERCIFUL SEA

The sky that day was a beautiful vivid blue,
she heard the sea babbling away like a waterfall,
frothing over a brook.
Abruptly the sky turned into the devil:
boisterous, rowdy anger,
with menacing black stormclouds rolling in
over the horizon.

The sea changed from good to bad,
just like a villainous villain.
Its jagged, jolting, juvenile ways had just
began to stir,
the violent monster of the waves came down
upon her head.

Amanda Strother (11)

RAVAGING SEA

It came out of the blue,
emerging swiftly towards the shore,
like a roaring contraption,
with hatred in its giant body,
devils controlling it like an
unbeatable robot.

It hurled relentlessly towards the cliffs,
infinite waves,
wildly demolishing anything that stood
in its path.
While incoming waves zigzagged
towards me, similar to a person in distress,
and wanted revenge.

Spitefully, it surged its way though
the green mercy ocean ruining the
beautiful landscape, suddenly it fired up,
terminating the rocks.
It started roaring infinitely, I just gave
up and the horrible creature destroyed the beautiful surroundings,
the sea reached out and pulled me
towards its mercy depths.

Daniel Waller (10)

THE CRUEL SEA

Cherry slipped down into seething rockpools,
The violent waves were dashing beside the cliff-face,
They hurled her into a surge of green froth,
And tossed her and tossed her whilst she gasped for air.

The waves were never-ending,
Cherry tried to call for help but her voice was
Strangled and suppressed by the wild waves,
They were crashing and thrashing and threatening,
And tucked Cherry away underneath the fierce froth.

She struggled for breath then finally,
The largest wave had come,
It towered over her like a gigantic building,
And that was the last she knew.

Claire Little (11)

THE GIANT'S NECKLACE

She walked along the sandy beach
Looking for the last thirty shells
She needed to finish the necklace
The clear blue sky suddenly changed
Black clouds came overhead
She knew
This was the menacing storm of anger.

The furious waves crashed against the cliff-face violently
The path ahead, was that the one?
She needed to get home
Then from the distance it came
The monster of the waves.

Sarah Treagus (10)

THE MENACING SEA

The menacing sea hurled its most
destructive waves at the defenceless rocks,
the tempestuous sea lashed at the shore,
finally the sea achieved what it desired,
the cliff began to lose the constant battle.

It reached out and swept up the small child,
cowering on the deserted shore,
the sea was pulling at her heals,
pulling, wrenching, dragging her back,
her body was being pulled and pushed,
turning this way and that like fish stuck in an angler's net.

The sea didn't care now,
nobody cared now.

The
sea
had
won.

Robin Binns (11)

THE SEA OF DEATH

So immersed in her search
Seeking 30 shells was she that day
The extreme ocean she did not see
But the baleful foghorn she heard

The grey bank of clouds rolled,
Moving remorsefully from the sea
White horses accumulated
Frantically she searched the clifftop

Cherry started to climb
Then one wave came and swept her off
'Mum, Dad! I'm home!' she cried
Sobbing they did not hear

Cherry was dead.

Benjamin Cardy (11)

THE CRUEL SEA

The bumpy shore hit the rocks like a
wailing whale surfing across the ocean.
The wet and windy waves bounced across
the sea and pulled the little girl towards the shore.
She rolled over on her back feeling
the salt-spray above her face.
A pair of raucous white gulls swooped
across her head.
The breaker crashed on the shore
from the jagged edge
and the battle started . . .

Tahli Carter (10)

THE GIANT'S NECKLACE

She rambled relentlessly on the shore,
She had to get those shells,
She needed only 30 more,
Where on earth were all those shells.

The boisterous, rowdy waves,
Came crashing to the shore,
They pulled at Cherry, pulled her,
Until she could hang on no more.

The never-ending battle
Of the sea, she was caught in,
She fought for freedom, fought it,
The sea seemed to never give in.

Eventually she faced it,
Her shells she reluctantly let go,
Cherry died tragically,
How? No one will ever know.

Vicki Young (10)

THE BREATH OF THE SEA

Cherry sat upon the beach,
Selecting only the best;
She didn't notice the rising storm,
The ever-increasing tempest.

At last she achieved her thirty goal,
It was time to retire home;
But to her horror and distress,
The sandy path had gone.

The next wave came,
It was only mild;
Clearing a path for
The lonely child.

She ran across the sliding rocks,
The monster she did not behold;
Burning, swelling out beyond,
Whirling like a tale untold.

Suddenly it was above her,
Towering above her shaken head;
It crushed her, and sucked her
And she was thrown away, cast down deep.
Dead.

Christopher Grimwood (10)

THE SEA TRAGEDY

Cherry was collecting shells,
Strolling along the golden shore,
The waves were bashing against the silver rocks,
Cherry didn't know she would live no more

The tempestuous white horse towered over her,
Making day turn to night,
While Cherry was running with her shells to her chest,
She was quivering with heart-shaking fright.

Cherry clambered up the rocks,
To avoid the torrential sea,
But it smashed viciously at her,
Cherry drowned slowly but eventually.

Andrew Nankivell (10)

PEOPLE

Take some love,
Some kindness too.
Leave out hatred,
Fighting too.
Add some sharing,
Some caring too.
Forget the anger,
And the rage.
Add some colour,
Pink, black, brown or yellow.

Mix it together and you have people.

Leo Jack (9)

SASSY

Sassy is my kitten's name,
biting feet is her favourite game.
Nothing will make her tame,
you would never call her a classy dame.

Charlotte Paull-Chorley (11)

THE SPELL

Boil, boil, trouble, trouble, in go all the ingredients
Bubble, bubble

Throw in the frogs' legs,
Throw in the smelly boy's toe,
Throw in the cheesy socks

Boil, boil, trouble, trouble, in go all the ingredients,
Bubble, bubble

Throw in the entrails of the animals,
Throw in the eye of a toad,
Throw in the poisonous skeleton

Boil, boil, trouble, trouble, in go all the ingredients,
Bubble, bubble.

Sadie Johnston (11)

BONFIRE

The scorching, blazing, blistering heat,
warming up the pitch-black night.
Sparks, cracks, bangs from the brilliancy of the
colourful flames.
Yellow, orange, red, hopping up and down.
Ashes floating in the sky, the incredible light
blasting and blazing.
A squeal and a sharp whistle - the fire will
burn and burn forever.

Carrie Lee (11)

PHOBIA

I can't move when I see one
I hate it when they run around really fast
Their long legs
Their titchy bodies
The terrifying noise they make when they're crawling around
                                                    really fast

When they just stay there and stare at me
Their big, fat, hairy legs
Their huge, big fangs
Their poisonous bites.

So all you
spiders out
there . . .

Die!

Emma Gleeson (11)

THE WITCH'S SPELL

Tongue of dog,
Ear of hog,
Let this spell bubble and pop.

Wing of bat,
Whisker of cat,
Body of gnat,
Chair of where the dead man sat.

Tongue of dog,
Ear of hog,
Let this spell bubble and pop.

Leg of newt,
Eye of frog,
Scales of a mouldy snake,
Water from a green stagnant lake.

Tongue of dog,
Ear of hog
Let this spell bubble and pop.

Sarah Reavey (11)

CHRISTMAS TREE

Little children decorate the tree
that everybody wants to see.
Come and see these sparkling lights
come and see them on these dark, sweet nights.
Chocolate coins that are rich to eat
the Christmas tree is so nice and neat.
Flashing lights screaming out the good news
and my dad's in his chair drinking all the booze.
Lots of children filled with joy
looking under the tree at all their toys.

Philip Horrocks (11)

PHOBIA

You're standing on a wall,
It's too much to bear.
I try to scream
No, nothing comes out.
You're watching the ground go past,
The atmosphere is still.
Time has stopped.
I shiver down my spine.
Help!

Anne-Marie Grace Glyde (11)

The Calm, Blue Sea

The calm, blue sea, I must go and see,
the evening sunset is as beautiful as can be.
As I look over the sea at the sunset breaking,
the winds start blowing and the sails start shaking.

The calm, blue sea, I must go and see,
for the calling of the morning tide is inside me.
I must go down to the sea and sky,
it is something I would really love to buy.

The calm, blue sea, I must go and see,
so I can have on the beach a lovely picnic tea.
Whisk me away from town, to the seaside calm,
to the Caribbean so I can see the tall, green palms.

Peter Abrahams (11)

THE SEA

The sea, the sea is calling me
to come and see all the
beautiful things it has for me.

The roaring of the waves when a
storm breaks out, the song of the sea
as silent as can be, the calmness of
the sea waiting for me to crash,
bash and swim. The gentle sea lapping at
my feet.

The sea, the sea is calling me
to come and see all the beautiful
things it has for me.
Oh! How I wish I could see the sea.

Clair Anderson (11)

THE SEA

The sun shines down on the deep blue sea
the waves roar loud and speak to me
come in, come in and swim away they say
I can't resist the beautiful bay
I jump in the sea and the water covers me
I swim and splash in the bright blue sea.
It's cool and refreshing, salty and clean
it makes me feel light and free.

Kayleigh Jones (11)

THE SEA

The silent sea is like a ghost without a voice.
The tiny fishing boats are bobbing about on
the mirror-reflective ocean. The wind delicately
sweeps over the ocean's tip. Then ever so
suddenly, as if someone has woken it up, the
sea's waves start to get bigger and bigger, until
the boats are ripped from their moorings and
the whole ocean is like a huge, blue giant
playing with his new toys. The sea is a great
crashing typhoon crashing against the great
sea walls. Then suddenly everything is
silenced by the rising tide of darkness.

Neil Crowley (11)

MONDAYS

Mondays are boring, back to school,
be slaves of torture and not learning a thing at all.

Sloppy cabbage with plastic meat,
and demented rice pudding for lunch.

Then there's what the teachers call games in their old age,
anyway an hour till home time, still some suffering to go
Spelling, with words like *benevolently* that we don't even know.

Kierstan Lordan (11)

THICK SMOKE

T hick black smoke in my face
H ow do we face the human race?
I f we weren't here, where would we be?
C an we be destroying more than we see?
K icking, shouting, trying to run

S ome people see what others have done
M ost people will, some people won't
O thers will die, 'Stop it you don't'
K illing is sometimes up to pollution
E ach of us smoking, is not the solution.

Carla Sutherland (11)